DIVINE
PURPOSE OF
FINGERPRINTS

MAGDLEEN DAVIDSON

ISBN 979-8-88783-537-2

CONTENTS

ACKNOWLEDGEMENTS

A word of knowledge emanating from an inspired heart truly desires to impact the readers with a greater magnitude in times to come. Just as the small rudder has the force to change the direction of a huge ship, so the word of knowledge has the power to change the direction of life.

I bow in reverence before my beloved **Lord Jesus Christ**, who has brought me this far.

I sincerely thank my **Holy Spirit**, who enabled me to know the revelation and pen my words.

My heartfelt respect and honour go to my parents, whose sacrifice blossomed into a legacy. I dedicate a heartfelt tribute to my dearest father, and I salute my dearest mother, **Jaisely Davidson**. She is the epitome of my spiritual strength and life. I thank my dearest sister, **Gracee Davidson**, for being a continual source of guidance and inspiration.

My sincere thanks to **Pastor Brian** and **Aunt Rosebell** for being very supportive.

I extend my heartfelt gratitude to **Reverend Brother Jose Malana**, the best principal I have ever met. He transforms the ordinary into the extraordinary. His trust and support have galvanised me to rise above the ordinary, and I remain indebted to him.

I am exceedingly grateful to **Madam Elizabeth Ashley**. She is the greatest blessing in my life. Her ingenuity has illumined me beyond measure, and I remain indebted to her.

I extend my gratitude to **Teacher Latika Fernandes**. Her priceless contribution, i.e. editing my compilation, is worth the admiration. She is a powerful driving force who makes things happen.

My heartfelt thanks to **Ms. Priya Faleiro**, who characterised and configured the entire text. Her invaluable contribution will always be treasured. Her humility and readiness to help are highly esteemed.

I am grateful to **Ms. Jeslina Fernandes**. Her benign qualities are worth appreciating.

I also thank **Ms. Rinal Fernandes**, who has always helped me accomplish my task.

I thank all my teachers for being very supportive and loving.

CHAPTER 1

FINGERPRINTS: YOUR UNIQUE IDENTITY

> *"God sealeth up the hand of every man so that all men may know His work."*
>
> Job 37:7

Francis Galton, a Victorian-era polymath, discovered that no two fingerprints are exactly alike and remain constant throughout the individual's life.

It is also known that he created a method for classifying fingerprints that proved useful in forensic science. It is scientifically proven that even identical twins do not have the same fingerprints, though they share their DNA code.

Johann Mayer, a German anatomist, was the first European to recognise that fingerprints are unique to each individual.

The present world population is approximately about eight billion, and just as the universe is expanding with discoveries each day, so is the human population growing exponentially.

Despite the growing population,

"You are set apart."

You are uniquely one creation who cannot be compared with anyone in this world.

Even if you were taken to the ancient past, Adam would say, **"You are uncommon."**

Your fingerprints have never matched and will never match with the fingerprints of the people at large as long as the earth sustains life.

Henry Faulds, a Scottish doctor, scientist and pioneering researcher of modern-day fingerprint technology, too suggested that the fingerprint of every individual is **unique**.

He examined the hands of infants and children to see if growth affected the fingerprint pattern. In his study, he found that even with severe peeling of the skin, the fingerprints will not change.

When the foetus moves, its growing fingers rub against the side of the womb. These little forces push the skin to mould in the direction of the growing ridges. Gradually, unique fingerprints are formed.

The fingerprint pattern is coded underneath the skin's surface, thus it cannot be destroyed or altered.

Fingerprints are distinct impressions that are left behind. In other words, whatever we touch, we leave behind the impressions of the ridges and lines that are so uniquely formed on our fingers.

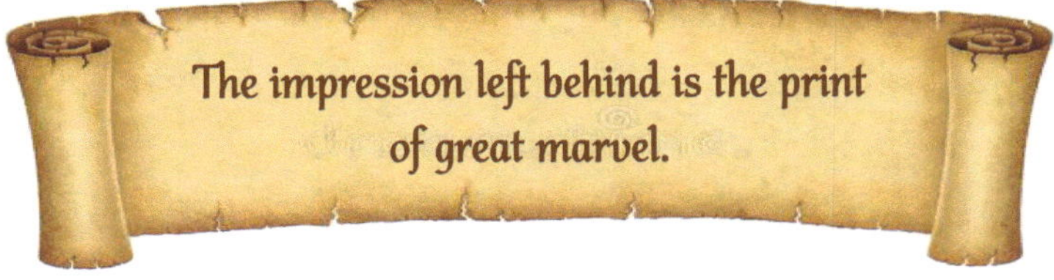

CHAPTER 2

BEHOLD THE UNIQUE CREATION

For a moment, let's muse over the mesmerising beauty of flowers, whose tender existence is truly captivating. Indeed it captures our hearts with admiration.

Even **William Wordsworth**, one of the greatest English poets who inaugurated the Romantic age, expressed…

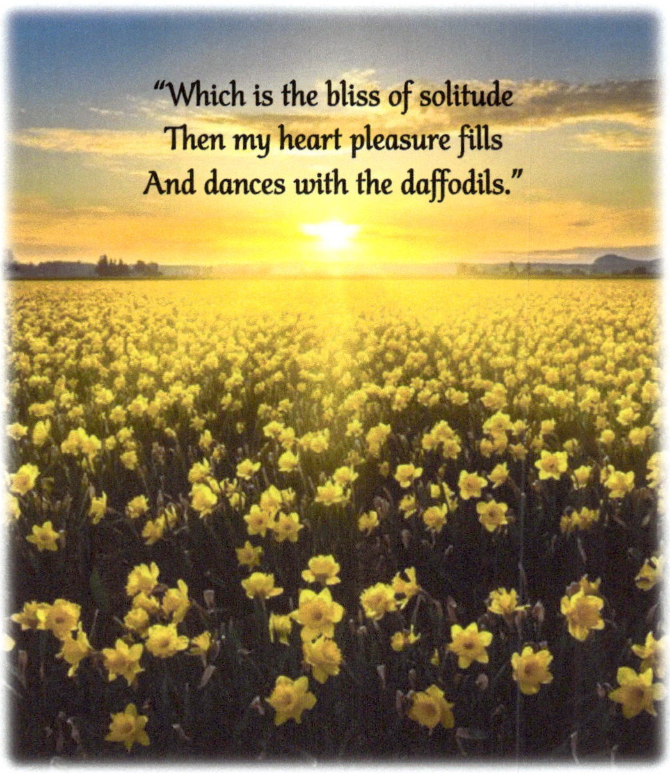

The endless view of the golden daffodils in a field across the lake filled the poet's heart with such rapturous joy that he relived the enthralling moment all his life and transformed his experience into resplendent lines.

No one can escape its beauty.

When we pass by the valley that stretches along the vast expanse of tender lilies, we cannot but stop ourselves and pour out our hearts with admiration. And while reflecting on its intricate beauty, the immaculate blossoms with divine fragrance allure us to paint the canvas of our hearts, embellishing the inspiration and the pleasure drawn from the striking creation of God.

When these flowers, which exist today and are scorched tomorrow, have such magnifying effect on the human soul, **Human beings make a greater impact with distinct characteristics – fingerprints being the classic identity with wonder-working power.**

Another alchemy of nature:

When a grain of sand gets into an oyster's shell, it secretes a substance called 'nacre' to seal the intruder. In course of time, the continuous process results in the formation of a **pearl.**

The oyster transforms the intruder into a priceless pearl. It makes the ordinary extraordinary.

Something to think about:

Small, frail and tender grass have the tenacity to conquer the solitude of the desert, and above all, they sustain the raging thunderstorm, while huge, sturdy trees have a great fall.

When these creations have such wonder-working power, the creation of man has greater magnitude – **a unique creation created in the image of God.**

When you begin to understand the chief purpose of your fingerprints, the whole gamut of your existence will become meaningful and worthy. Undoubtedly, there will be a paradigm shift moving from uncertainty to certainty, experiencing the buoyant confidence that was never felt before.

CHAPTER 3

A CLASSIC STORY OF 'PRAYING HANDS'

'**Praying Hands**', a masterpiece sketched by the renowned **German Renaissance artist, Albrecht Durer**, won overwhelming acclamation worldwide.

There's an unforgettable account embedded in the incomparable sketch. Albrecht Durer and Albert wanted to pursue their dreams – their potential talent for art. Financial constraints thwarted their pursuit and almost buried them under the hardships of life.

However, the determined artists created a workable plan. It was decided that one would work and give financial support to the other to attend the art academy. In effect, they tossed a coin on one beautiful Sunday morning after the church service.

Albrecht Durer won the toss and, according to the plan, left for Nuremberg, whereas Albert went to the old mines to work as a labourer.

After four long years, Albrecht Durer returned, completing his graduation in art. His family welcomed him with triumphant celebration. Soon after dinner, which resonated with soft music, Albrecht slowly rose to his feet and said, "Albert, it is your turn. Now, you go to embark upon your mission and fulfil your dreams."

The words deeply touched Albert's heart and tears streamed down his face. He thanked Albrecht and said, "Thank you for giving me the opportunity, but it's too late. Now my fingers are no longer slender and flexible. I cannot even make a delicate line on the canvas with a brush."

Albrecht was deeply touched and was determined to express his heartfelt gratitude in a way that would be memorable. He wanted to take it at large to make the whole world know the selfless love of Albert who sacrificed his dream for his brother.

Being deeply motivated, the renowned artist was ready for a remarkable creation. Albrecht drew 'Praying Hands' in honour of Albert's love and sacrifice.

It is conceived that Albrecht called the piece of drawing simply 'Hands'. But the world at large was awestruck and renamed the sketch **'Praying Hands'**.

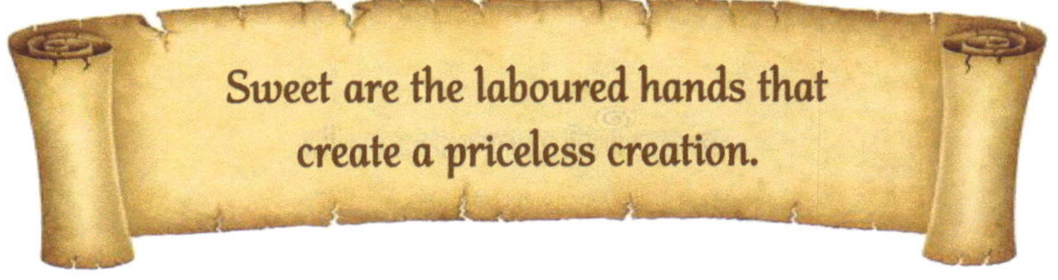

CHAPTER 4

SYNERGY OF FINGERPRINTS

Digging deep

At first, one gets a feeling that it is an appealing story of love and sacrifice. Indeed it is. However, there is also an untold truth beyond it.

Albert readily accepted his part to work in the mines without regret and never languished even for a moment. He worked faithfully engaging himself in the hard task of labour and, at the same time, guarded his heart with all diligence. It wasn't easy for him to remain in this state consistently. Nevertheless, he persevered and remained steadfast in his mind and laboured ceaselessly.

It is believed that every day with perpetual continuity he laboured in every difficult circumstance. Quite often he encouraged himself when he experienced the excruciating pain his fingers sensed. He stood his ground firm even when he saw the transformation of his beautiful, slender fingers to being hard, gnarled and twisted; the shattering of his dreams.

How did he guard his heart in such circumstances? What caused him to remain steadfast?

Indeed Albert stands apart teaching us a lesson about life.

Albert's fingerprints resonated well with his diligent heart, leaving an indelible mark on his labour that emanated from his fingerprints.

Remember, he was not pursuing his dream and had to pay a very high price. Nevertheless, he stayed determined and calm and guarded his heart, which made his hands move like a whirlwind, exploiting every moment to the optimum.

A perfect resonance was getting ready for the extraordinary which Albert never dreamt of. Albrecht, with his slender fingers, created an exceptional masterpiece, but Albert's hard, gnarled hand created an epoch to prove that any work done with a resonated synergy of fingerprints and a well-guarded heart begets the uncommon. It's only a matter of time and will be definitely realised.

When I look intently at the sketch, 'Praying Hands', I am astounded to realise that the hands that laboured diligently never ceased to pray.

The sketch of 'Praying Hands' has a deeper implication.

The hands that are lifted in prayer lift the divine purpose of fingerprints; an act of reverence – submitting oneself into the Hands of the Almighty.

When the outward gesture comes from the inward conviction, heartfelt prayer becomes an incense reaching the throne of God.

"For the eyes of the Lord move to and fro throughout the earth that He may strongly support those whose heart is completely His."

2nd Chronicles 16:9

When people look up to the sketch, 'Praying Hands', not only Albrecht's masterstroke but also Albert's masterwork is impressed in their minds permanently.

People gaze at Albrecht's masterpiece with admiration and look up to Albert's laboured hands with adoration – **indeed a tribute to Albert**.

The synergy between diligent hands and a well-guarded heart tailors life and inspires the lives of many.

CHAPTER 5

THE WONDER-WORKING POWER OF YOUR FINGERPRINTS

Did you know?

Fingerprints are formed at the same time as the brain's neocortex, which controls our emotions and cognitive abilities.

During the early days, American doctors discovered an unusual case of a newborn baby without a brain. The absence of the brain was associated with the absence of fingerprints. Such reported cases led medical experts to believe that the brain is linked to fingerprints.

With extensive research, medical experts substantiated that the brain and human fingerprints form and develop between the 13th and 21st week. So, a scientific relationship between fingerprints and the brain was established.

It is concluded that through the study of fingerprints, a lot more could be unravelled about the functioning of the brain.

With the help of the **'Imaging Technique'**, researchers confirm that even the structural connections of the brain are unique to each individual.

Thus human intelligence, emotions and fingerprints form a structured circuit.

Neurobiologists claim that with a such link between fingerprints and the cerebral cortex, human intelligence is bound to reflect from the fingerprint pattern.

If there is a relationship between fingerprints and the profound physiological function of the brain, how valuable is the apparent purpose of our fingerprints?

Breaking down further, the connection between our emotions and fingerprints can bring a revolutionary change once its purpose is realised.

Almighty God has seen our **unformed substance** while in our mother's womb and has pronounced life to us. How much more can we thrive when our **formed substance** surrenders to the will of God?

CHAPTER 6

EMOTIONAL RESONANCE

David Hawkins, MD, PhD, proved that emotions have measurable energy and impact our cells.

Hawkins, in his book, *Power versus Force*, explains that a person's measurable energy level in their magnetic field increases when that person is experiencing positive or divine emotions.

One of the most interesting findings was that cells died when the log level was below 200. In simpler terms, when emotions such as hate, anxiety, despair and humiliation are active, the log level is below 200.

Hertz Vibration Scale shows that when a person is experiencing peace, joy, empathy, love, confidence, self-control or faith, they have the energy to remain indefatigable in any situation.

The Holy Bible says that the heart is the wellspring of life.

The heart is a powerful source that overflows with thoughts, words and actions.

In the Jewish vernacular, the heart is the seat of emotions, and their common greeting is **'Shalom'** which means **peace**.

The Jews believe that the heart sees, hears, rejoices, comforts and sorrows. They also believe that the goodness of an individual, which is reflected in speech and conduct, directly relates to **"lev tov"** which means **"good heart"**. The commandments of the Lord are genuinely impressed in their hearts.

The Jews are deeply rooted in their beliefs. Thus most of the iconic names emerge from the Jewish community. Albert Einstein invented modern physics, Isaac Asimov defined the laws of robotics and Rosalind Franklin, a renowned chemist, discovered the molecular structure of DNA. Three-quarters of Jewish ancestry have been awarded the Nobel Prize, accounting for 22% of all the individual recipients worldwide between 1901 and 2021.

Despite being under attack for centuries, the resilient Jewish people have always risen above the onslaught. Their unwavering, grounded beliefs and their fortified determination caused many to rise to their calling. Thus their inventions and discoveries are notable, which include the laser, genetic engineering, Cholera vaccine, Polio vaccine, Google and so on.

The secret of their success beyond measure is their good heart holding on to the scriptural teachings and living by the teachings wholeheartedly.

The connection between the well-guarded heart and the divine purpose of the fingerprints is ready for the extraordinary.

The work accomplished is not common. It may seem ordinary during the course, but it becomes extraordinary when endured.

In contrast, when we are in a sufferable state of unforgiveness, fear, anxiety, bitterness, anger or pride, we are pulled to the lowest ebb.

Toxic Emotions

This state is unfavourable as it affects our work, relationships and health directly or indirectly.

Neither our work nor our relationships will hold the vital dynamism, i.e. the energy or the power.

"You (God) created my inmost being, You knit me together in my mother's womb."

Psalm 139: 13

"I praise You because I am fearfully and wonderfully made. Your works are wonderful, I know that fully."

Psalm 139:14

CHAPTER 7

FINGERPRINTS: AN INDELIBLE BRIDGE

The fingerprint is a bridge that connects your emotional state to your work and relationships.

Fingerprints are immutable and unchanging. The seal on our fingers is wonder-working.

God Almighty, in His sovereignty, created each one of us so uniquely different that each person has the potential to rise to his/her calling.

But this calling does not manifest the way it should because the surpassing purpose of the beautiful connection between the well-guarded heart and the fingerprints is unknown.

"Guard your heart with all diligence for out of it springs the issues of life."

Proverbs 4:23

Your heart is the seat of your beliefs. Your established beliefs drive you to actions, and your actions become a way of life.

Your beliefs drive you to action, and your action determines your achievement. Right beliefs lead to right living because now there is a vision that makes you limitless.

The divine purpose of fingerprints does not change, but the condition of the heart is unstable and convulsive most of the time.

Sometimes we are high and at other times we are low, as far as our feelings are concerned. Inadvertently, we become like those raging waves that cannot stay calm. Above all, the loud, innumerable voices in our minds make us sick and depraved. We feel completely defeated or rather weak in the face of challenges or situations.

In course of time, we realise that more than the distressing situations and circumstances that seemingly surface now and then, the unstable condition of the heart is our burden.

The fingerprints do not resonate with evil or unstable hearts. One cuts oneself from the divine purpose, and the resonated bridge is thwarted and blocked. A heart with evil intent or a depraved state of heart has a serious impact on work and relationships.

They continue to live their life either in reproach or misery, believing that they are destined to live such a life.

Basing one's life on this false belief, the individual disarrays his/her life to either living a compromised or superficial life.

Both are unacceptable.

Lord Jesus Christ beautifully said, "I have come to give you life, life in abundance to the full till it overflows."

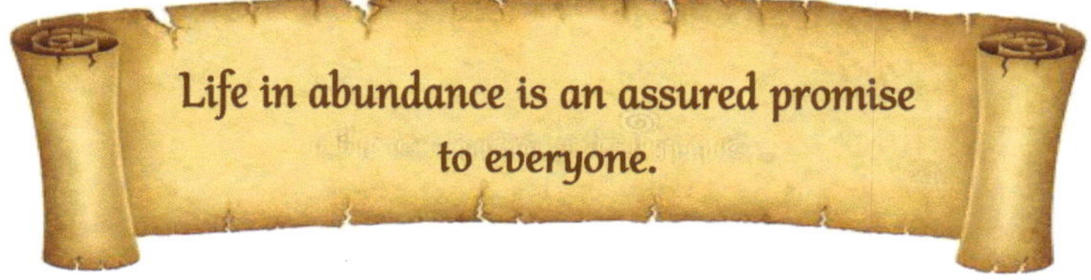

CHAPTER 8

THE HEART IS AT WAR

Our minds and emotions are always at work. With the passage of time, as we grow and mature, the impact of our experiences, which is the result of our belief system, is deeply rooted in the recesses of our minds.

Our beliefs shape our thinking, which in turn has an impact on our behaviour. Most of the time we don't examine our beliefs because we believe that our beliefs are true and undefiable.

We experience what we believe.

Since we have not guarded ourselves, as far as our belief system is concerned, we find ourselves in a distressful state for a long time. Both mind and heart become sick and desperate. Diligently, we begin to look out for ways in order to be delivered.

After an earnest search, we do find some ways and endeavour to adopt practical approaches, but sooner or later we realise that **heart is at war during this crucial time.**

Remember, the impact of your experiences, particularly those that have caused overwhelming affliction, has been deeply entrenched in your mind and heart.

Since we are desperate to be delivered, we begin to examine our beliefs and endeavour to address them. We turn onto a new leaf to believing what is right and true. While believing what is true, we realise that unbelief, which was once our belief, keeps resurfacing and is dismally active.

Let me illustrate…

The two horses named 'belief' and 'unbelief' indisputably standing in the opposite direction are trying to pull the load apart.

Will the load budge?

The two horses are proving their strength at the same time in the opposite direction.

The strength of belief and unbelief are at work. In other words, good thoughts and feelings and negative thoughts and their corresponding feelings exert force alternately.

You are believing yet unbelieving.

We do believe what is right and true, but at the same time deep within our hearts, we feel the negative force of unbelief at work.

It's quite appalling. This kind of perplexed state is intriguing and should not be overlooked.

Belief and unbelief can have their forces at the same time, leaving one more confused and dismayed.

The paradoxical presence of belief and unbelief leads to volatile frustration, driving one to make wrong decisions. Like the hamster on the wheel, we find ourselves whirling around the issues of life continuously, and the solutions seem to be a remote possibility.

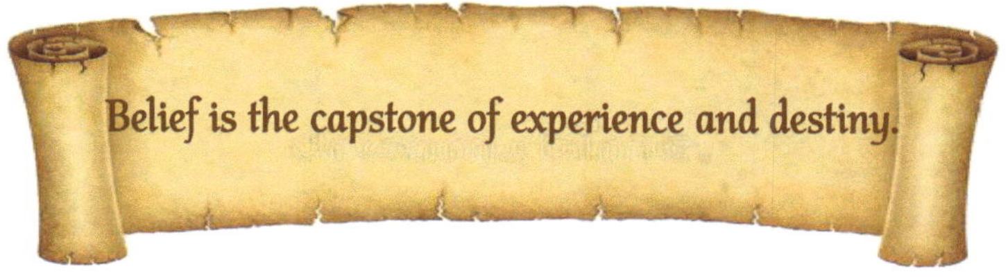

CHAPTER 9

BREAKING THE CHAIN

When true beliefs set in and the old beliefs that are not based on truth have not been vanquished, the incongruous presence of the old and new beliefs continue to dwell, making one stagnant. Deep fatigue sets in, causing physical strain and mental blocks.

There's only one practical solution to the problem, i.e. breaking the chain of old beliefs. We must make an earnest effort to invalidate those old beliefs that did not have the substance of truth and resist ourselves the outward expressions of unbelief such as complaining, accusing, criticising, fretting, lamenting, unyielding, unforgiving and rousing to anger.

One has to continually act on true beliefs and resist the unbeliefs that keep surging now and then. This resistance is not easy as it entails one to engage in a tough fight. Thus most people find it difficult and quit. But the one who perseveres is the victor.

Focus on your true beliefs because it gives you energy. Your true and empowering beliefs will begin to hold dynamism, and your unbeliefs will be weakened and finally defeated.

Life is never bed of roses. The storms of life will continue to rage against us until our last breath. The good news is that my boat will not sink as it has the buoyancy of true beliefs. Right beliefs strengthen us, not only to handle the storms of life lion-heartedly but also to be invincible.

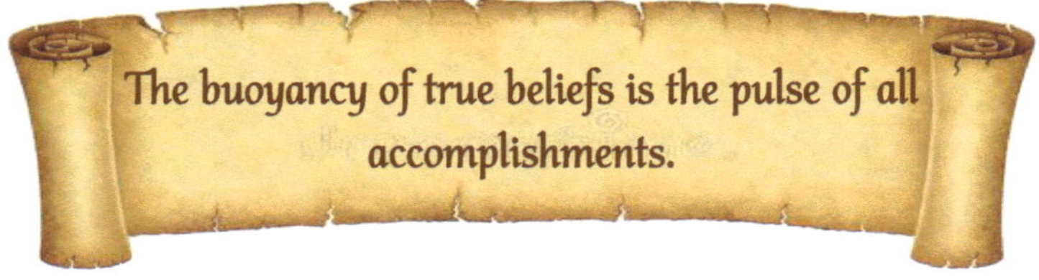

CHAPTER 10

THE HEALING OF YOUR HEART

Now one may argue that it has nothing to do with fingerprints and it's all about positive thinking.

Agreed, positive thinking does play a significant role, but you must also know that it is just a part of the synergetic resonance.

Breaking down further…

Just **remaining positive** may not help us reach our exceptional, desired destiny, and it may not heal us either. There is something more beyond.

This is the tipping point.

A person with positive thinking may not be doing the right thing **always**. Remember, his/her actions are influenced by his/her belief system that was already formed and is seated in his/her heart.

There are innumerable evidence showing that the individuals who were strong and undeniably positive could not endure long. They either failed and receded in the background, unable to rise again or brought an end to themselves.

What is the purpose of changing the thought and not the state of the heart?

The toxic emotions are dismally rooted, and the issues of life continue to overwhelm us.

You may try to bring about a change by changing your thoughts but will not endure long.

The reason is that **you fail to address your heart**, which is an important part of emotions and feelings. Despite changing our thought process, we continue to feel the vacuum as peace is missing, inner joy is lost, faith has weakened, forgiveness is not existing and confidence has departed.

You change your thoughts without addressing your heart, which is seared with toxic emotions.

You wonder why despite thinking positive, nothing changes in your life. Eventually, you end up surrendering yourself to your former ways.

Many times we endeavour to think positive but suppress our deep-rooted emotions and feelings. When things don't work, we become frustrated and depressed.

The embittered heart harms our work, productivity, relationships and health. Above all, such a state of the heart does not synergise with our fingerprints. Thus the work done does not hold dynamism.

First thing first… change your belief system. Begin to believe what is right and true in the eyes of God Almighty. Make an earnest effort to enrich your heart with divine emotions. When divine emotions become the seat of your heart, you begin to think about what is good and positive. Eventually, the new you, the best you, emerges from within, and you become **unique**.

The desired change does not happen overnight.

Let me tell you a true story of a beautiful mother, Susanna, who was born in 1669 in England. She was instrumental in bringing about a revolutionary change in the world.

She had nineteen children but nine died in infancy. She suffered as her husband, Samuel, was overwhelmed with stringent, poor financial abilities. He would be away from home for days and couldn't take care of his family. Financial deprivation debilitated Susanna and her ten children with continual struggle. Added to their misery, their house was burnt twice. After the second fire, Susanna was forced to keep her children in different homes. She struggled indefinitely and worked hard to restore everything that was lost.

She took her relationship with God as seriously as she did her duties. In the early days of her life, she vowed that she would never spend more time in leisure and entertainment and devoted her time to prayer, Bible study and work.

The devoted mother would place her Bible on her favourite chair and put on her long apron over her head, forming a kind of a tent, just like the tabernacle in the days of the old testament. And she would prepare herself before the Lord earnestly with Bible study and prayer for more than two hours. At that time, all her children would remain solemnly quiet. The children were obedient because they were disciplined.

Against all odds, she succeeded in giving her children a good education. They all learnt Latin and Greek and were tutored in the classical studies that were traditional in England at that time.

The stressful circumstances that kept mounting put a lot of strain on her life. She had every reason to be dismayed and broken. She could hear the shrieks of failure and defeat deep in her mind and around her, but indomitably she refused to be apprehensive and fearful.

Guarding her heart, she forcibly entered into her new realm, causing Heaven to open the floodgates of blessings upon her.

Her son, John Wesley, rose to be the founder of the Methodist Church, and Charles Wesley became the most prolific English poet for composing more than 6500 hymns.

All her children rose to their calling.

The mother created a vision beyond her dreams.

Willingness to change is the foundation; long endurance in the face of critical circumstances is the framework. Pacing ahead with the same magnitude despite the trials of life is the architectural blueprint;

remaining steady with a well-guarded heart is the defeat of gravity that pulls you down, and divine destiny is your accomplishment.

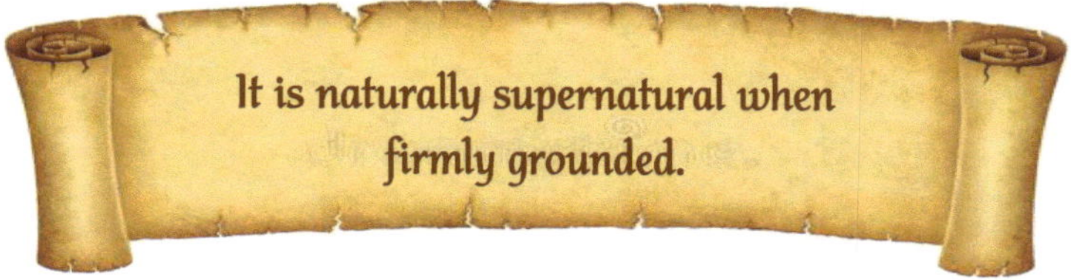

CHAPTER 11

THE POWER OF ENDURANCE

The Dead Sea, also called the Salt Sea, is a landlocked salt lake between Israel and Jordon in southwestern Asia.

It has a very high salt content, and nothing survives in it. It is below the mean sea level, and there are no outlet streams. In the absence of the outlet, the water that evaporates continuously leaves behind a large amount of salt. Thus life cannot exist here.

When despair and gloom persist for a long period, toxic emotions and their effects begin to deepen, and we find ourselves trapped in the gory darkness of issues.

The Sea of Galilee is just the north of Dead Sea. Both the Sea of Galilee and the Dead Sea receives water from River Jordon. Unlike the Dead Sea, the Sea of Galilee thrives with plants and marine life because it has outlet streams.

When we are engulfed with distress, we have to find the outlet that will keep us on course.

And that outlet is to position ourselves to be undefeated, remain anchored in hope and be driven by true beliefs. Such a developed character will diminish the bullheaded presence of despair.

The journey of life is never without trials and tests. Its intensity and origin may vary from person to person and may tarry for some time.

When severely afflicted, we find it difficult to remain unaffected and may be pulled down to the lowest ebb by the vortex of issues. There is a raging storm within and a high tide outside.

This is the time we have to create a dividing line that will separate us from the gruesome darkness of hopelessness.

The blessed beauty of life is that when we decide to endure the trials patiently with great expectation, an untold staying power emerges from within us, capacitating us to stay on course.

Keep reminding yourself that God Almighty has sealed your palms and He knows everything about you from the beginning. God is the author of your life; so don't quit.

Many history-makers rose from this enduring journey to make exceptional contributions.

When you deepen yourself with hope and endurance, God will broaden your horizon.

CHAPTER 12

THE SECRET BEAUTY OF RESONANCE

Dr. John Dewey stated, "The deepest urge in human nature is the desire to be important."

True, everyone longs to be important and desires that his/her work should be of paramount importance and worth recognition. We do engage ourselves in proving our mettle daily. We do endeavour earnestly to exploit our potential to the optimum.

Despite our earnest attempts, we feel the untold vacuum in us as the work may have not produced its desired results. Even if it is achieved, it may have not reached its commendable juncture of greater impact. This is because we have derailed from the resonance of a well-guarded heart and the divine purpose of fingerprints.

A feeling of despair that had birthed keeps looming in the distressing loom of discontentment and despair.

A yarn is indeed spun but has an invisible print of anguish, anger and distraught at the same time.

Our work, which is like a yarn, is complete in its character but is invisibly scorched by the non-conjunction of the diligent heart and fingerprints.

The fingerprints conjunct with a diligent heart which has been nurtured with divine emotions, and its synergetic character produces the extraordinary.

When our heart is ingrained with toxic emotions, the pivotal role of the fingerprints is detached.

The divine purpose of fingerprints gets concealed; thus our work does not hold the divine impression.

Remember, heart is the prime seat not only of our emotions but also of **our will**.

God Almighty does not bypass our will. Right from the inception of our world, He has never bypassed any human's will including Adam's and Eve's.

Our fingerprint, which is the **seal of God**, is the **will of God** and is unchangeable. When we make a conscious effort to guard our hearts, we locate ourselves at the centre of the will of God and experience the divine purpose of fingerprints.

When the seal of God (fingerprints) conjuncts with a well-guarded heart (will of God), we move from strength to strength to our destined destination, which is so beautifully planned by our God Almighty.

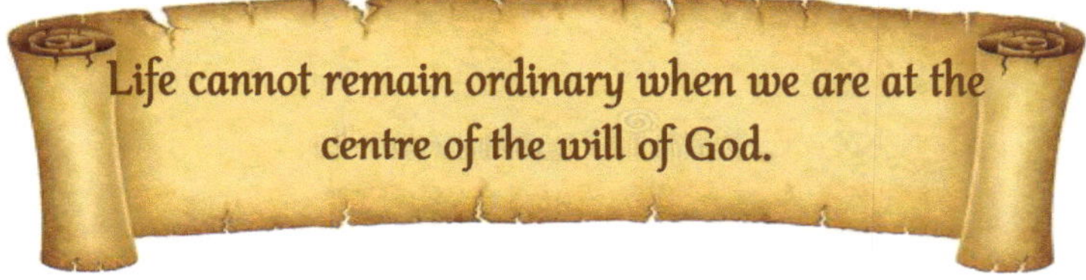

ACCEPT GOOD OR BAD WITH GRATITUDE

Once when the narrator visited her friend on one occasion, she saw beautiful flowering plants at her residence. The most beautiful of all was the golden chrysanthemum that bloomed in all its intricate beauty. But it was growing in an old, rusty pot. Her friend said that she ran out of pots, knowing that the beautiful blossom would not mind growing in a dented pot.

Immediately, she reflected upon the life of the old fisherman.

One evening, when the narrator was making supper, there was a knock at the door. She opened it and saw an awful-looking man with a shrivelled body. The narrator who lived directly across the street near John Hopkins Hospital in Baltimore rented the upstairs rooms to the out-patients.

At first, she hesitated to let him in, but his convincing words mellowed her.

After dinner, the narrator decided to spend some time with the old fisherman who was playing merrily with her children. She learnt that he fished for his living and supported his daughter, her five children and her husband who was hopelessly crippled from a back injury. The old man himself suffered from a kind of skin cancer and was undergoing treatment at John Hopkins Hospital.

While he was sharing his story, she was deeply moved and realised that the old gentleman did not complain even for a moment. He always prefaced his statements by thanking the Lord. "Thank God, I can work despite my old age and take care of my beautiful family. I thank God as I don't suffer much physical pain."

The old gentleman continued to work diligently and guarded his heart against all odds. Apparently, his work began to hold dynamism, and he was getting ready for something extraordinary.

At the end of the excerpt, the narrator made an exceptional statement. God might have said when He came to the soul of the sweet fisherman that He won't mind dwelling in his small, weak body.

(An Excerpt from an article from the Times of India.)

It is believed that this particular excerpt was read by thousands and may have been inspired. One of the reviewers wrote that she had read many articles but this one was unparalleled.

The fact that many were inspired is a beautiful tribute to the old, sweet gentleman.

What greater purpose of life is there than to inspire the lives of many?

CHAPTER 14

THE SUPERNATURAL POWER OF TRUE BELIEFS

The sweet, old gentleman had all the reasons to complain and lament over his grievous conditions. Even the little comforts of life did dread to visit him.

He struggled all his life and had innumerable legitimate questions like others. When he should have been taken care of he took care of his family without any complaints. He had every reason to be sorrowful and complain but he refused to do so.

On the contrary, he kept nurturing his heart with peace, joy and gratitude, this beautiful attitude separated him from others at large. Even the heavens were captivated by his attitude.

He did not have the comfort, luxury, fame and wealth, but what he had was the dynamism that changed the perception of many – **the rarest phenomenon.**

Empowering beliefs ignite vision, which is a road map to our destiny. It helps us overcome the roadblocks and hurdles of life and enables us to anchor our hope. Above all, it capacitates us to remain steadfast amid trials and adversity.

When we inch closer to our destiny, the invisible becomes uniquely visible; a beautiful truth of life that began with the first step of true belief

We have to shift the paradigm and relocate ourselves by acting on our beliefs and remaining still in the face of trials.

Being still in the face of tribulations is the fiercest battle that we can live through but when braved confidently, we shall bear the fruit of our service in due season.

Above all, an endured heart attracts the impression of the fingerprints, creating momentum for an outstanding manifestation.

As penned earlier, it is a matter of time. One has to wait until the fullness of time.

When you plant and nurture a bamboo plant, you will not see anything visible in the first year. Even with constant nurture, you won't see any growth. The same condition prevails during the third and fourth years. But in the fifth year, you can see a spectacular sight – a dazzling visual treat. The bamboo tree has grown eighty feet tall in just six weeks. First four years, it was growing underground, getting rooted strong and deep.

Likewise, the strength of our true beliefs needs to be deeply rooted and nurtured with the expressions of divine and empowering emotions.

Wait for the fullness of time until the invisible becomes visible.

CHAPTER 15

THE CENTRE AND THE CIRCUMFERENCES OF YOUR FINGERPRINTS

A devout Christian printed an image of a fingerprint and started tracing out each line intricately. He discovered that there are sixty-six lines; the exact number of books in the Bible.

In course of time, he began to assign each line of the fingerprints to its corresponding verse in the Bible. He persevered with this laborious task and meticulously studied and tried to connect each line of the fingerprints to its corresponding Bible verse.

In other words, each line has the impression of the word of God.

By implication, we understand that God does not separate His Word from us. He has etched our names on His palm.

He made us in His own image so that we cannot be separated from His Word.

Saint Bonaventure said, "We are the fingerprints of God."

He, who is called the second founder of the Franciscan Order, spoke of God as one whose centre is everywhere and circumference is nowhere.

As proof, this print is impressed on our fingers. Look closely at your fingerprints; it has the centre that defines the presence of God and the circumference that defines your destiny, which is so immeasurably expansive.

In my last strokes, I would like to reiterate that your fingerprint has your story etched by the hand of God. Therefore, the story is undoubtedly and incomparably beautiful. This defined story has to match your well-guarded heart, the headquarter of your emotions and your will. Once matched, you become **unstoppable**.